In the *Light* of Pure Love

Poems of Spiritual Inspiration

Karen Muller

Balboa Press books may be ordered through booksellers or by contacting:

Balboa Press
A Division of Hay House
1663 Liberty Drive
Bloomington, IN 47403
www.balboapress.com.au
1 (877) 407-4847

ISBN: 978-1-5043-1643-9 (sc)
ISBN: 978-1-5043-1644-6 (e)

Print information available on the last page.

Balboa Press rev. date: 01/25/2019

BALBOA
PRESS
A DIVISION OF HAY HOUSE

This book in dedicated to my darling girl,

Amber Reynolds

27.07.77 to 03.11.14.

My greatest teacher.

Poetry

Written By Karen Muller (Reynolds)

1979 — 2018

Acrostic

Remembering

Emotions

Inner depths of

Numbed awareness forming tears

Cascading freely from

An age-old being

Releasing

Negativity

Affecting

To reflect

Instances that

Once before and once again

Nurture profound understanding

Cinquain

SKY

CLEAR BLUE

INFINITE BEAUTIFUL ALWAYS

ASTONISHING WONDER

HIGH

4

Haiku

Dewdrops swell and flow
Golden dawn sunshine glitters
To nurture fresh growth.

Willows streams bamboo
Flow and sway to wisps of breeze
Beautiful soft tune.

Gull circling high
Floating freely sees below
With a beady eye.

Spirit Dance

Written by Karen Muller
August 2018

No more ills as your spirit soars

Through the air in total rapport

Twist and turn in a ballet dance

Of gypsy heart you twirl and prance

No more holding back in time

Your purpose now a joyous rhyme

Flow with ecstatic jubilant release

Your soul has found enduring peace

Meander to fall into graceful steps

That rotates with others into joyful leaps

You feel yourself in your total being

And see meaning in the life you were living

You continue to learn as your life goes on

Though you pirouette to a different tune

Like a butterfly evolves and a flower blooms

Your individuality blossoms with every move

Softly you step into your ultimate self

Released from earthly pain and doubt

Wonderment embraces heavens motion

Freedoms is the gift and love is the devotion.

Amber's Poem
Written by Karen Muller
February 2018

When you died I realised how short life is, how precious each day is and each day
I have an obligation to live this day to the best of my ability.

For that day, each and every day brings me a step closer to our reunion although each day I know and honour you are with me.

I found out that I did not only love you with all my heart.

I found out I love you with all my soul too.

How very special is each memory from our time here together and each day that we can still create memories from the many occurrences that prove you are so very alive. You are more alive than I.

How poignant it is to me, how much you suffered, your immense pain from such difficult and tragic events in your life that have been shared with me.

My heart broke for you and my heart was restored with each and every time you regained yourself and your joy. It still does..

For you always, always love so deeply..

Love that no time or death can lessen, your love only continues to grow in strength.

My darling girl, you are my ultimate teacher.

You continue to give me strength, fascination, delight, joy, depth, insight, courage, wisdom, purpose, hope, faith, inspiration and meaning amidst the pain.

Ultimately, the power of your love, shines ever brightly upon me. Your light bathes in the truth and meaning of living.

Mum

Trance

Written by Karen Muller (Reynolds)
1985

Life
an illusion, a reality, a vibration, inter-dimensional, universal
creation.

I
with partial vision see awareness tangled through an incomprehensible
infinite cosmic network. Cause and effect a dimension within itself,
orbiting, enmeshing through time past, now and time to come.

Perception,
life as I write... thoughts... fraction and divert....create and
control action.... influential essence. I sense vibration echoes as
I am obvious of my surroundings intuitively.

Awareness

Written by Karen Muller (Reynolds)

1988

My
loving soul soars over the land weaving with the songs, the grace of
the golden wind.
Sweet
luminous perfumes emanate from invisible flowers, hypnotising.
Red
earth winding, mesmerising.
The
wonder of feelings as we greet.
Entwining
webs of freedom.
Strengthening,
understanding, depths of compassion.
Vast
as the cosmos..........................
Radiating
forever in an inter-relation of the ecstatic glowing beauty of being.

Breeze

Written by Karen Muller (Reynolds)

August 1984

Gentle
wind weaves and sweeps amidst the trees
In
passing healing, drying broken leaves
Whispering
caressing in early morning hours
Cooling,
soothing swirling with power
Meandering,
moving creating tears
To
cry upon ground for countless years

Death

Written By Karen Muller (Reynolds)
1994

As now the sun is setting in the purple velvet sky
the birds have ceased their singing tucked in cosy nests on high
The stars begin appearing, their twinkling, growing ever bright
Clouds cast shadows on the moon, as slowly they move by
The uniqueness of this day that is passing has gathering to become
night
For that day that has been living, like everything was
born to die
And in the peaceful darkness that is still vibrantly alive
the bonds of endless love endure
and return like morning light.

Starvation

Written by Karen Muller (Reynolds)

1985

Ethiopia

My brother your pain so deep I felt

I was distraught, ashamed with guilt

Seeing you starve with savage cruelty

Knowing your funds are making people more money

Aware that your children die in your arms

With wars raging it so alarms

How can the people so openly know

Your babes die just like the crop you have sown

I witness the lies and the conceit

and the empty values were lead to believe

Plastic movie land has the importance of being

more important than you and your loved ones living.

Candle Meditation
Written by Karen Muller (Reynolds)
January 1990

The candle flame burns as I meditate
on thoughts of you,

no time, no distance only the essence of truth.

I send the feeling, bonds of love waves that caress

The magical depth of created intent.

To reach, for you to be aware

I'm entwine through your soul deliciously bare.

The wick of fire burns

Reminding of what is special,

Rekindling within, stirrings essential

held between each other's hearts.

As physical distance bids that we part.

Sacred is the flame that strengthens our ties.

Dedicated are the hours that pass us by

and blessed are we able to unite

Through belief and trust

through passion, through life's

Enduring love light.

Interconnection

By Karen Muller (Reynolds)

1979

Another day is over
The night is very young
The mystery and the starkness
Make feelings more alone
My thoughts wander aimlessly
They catch upon the wind
Then fade with their intensity
Wisps of breeze softly mend
I was feeling insecure
I was missing friendly touch
But on this gentle warm night
Every thing is such
What I feel like giving
Is held within my heart
Waiting for that someone
To become a special part
Of a life lived together
To bask in the depth of love
That meaning tempts to promise
With fulfilment of life's chart

Meanwhile as I am waiting
For that someone to arrive
What is held within me
Is not suppressed or starved
In awe and admiration
I look around and see
Water reflects silver moon beams
That glint so liberally
And within this duration
Indigo shadows of the trees
Show their glowing aural light
Glimmering so free
Here surrounded by nature
I feel vigorously alive
How could I ever begin to have
Feelings of being deprived
When I stop to recognise
All that surrounds me
We share this life and life force
How blessed in beauty are we.

In The Light of Pure Love

Written By Karen Muller

March 2018

From when we are born we seek to survive
In a span of unpredictable time.
We enter when our body expires
Into the realm of the other side
In the light of pure love..

Our actions, our thoughts our feelings all feed
Into what know and choose to believe
As the karmic wheel turns
What we give we receive
In the light of pure love..

When your time here ends
What will your life mean?
Do you give freely to others, those in need?
Or does materialism seek to appease your greed?
In the light of pure love..

Do you deeply care for your fellow man?
Or are you blissfully ignorant, your head in the sand?
Are you sufficiently poised to make a stand?
To shield the defenceless or lend a hand?
In the light of pure love..

Can you stand proud of who you've become?
Feel unafraid and never alone?
All the result of the deeds you have done
And the behaviour you've shown
In the light of pure love..

Is your worth based in simple honour and truth?
Or do you lie, cheat and corrupt or abuse?
Under the delusion that some or non knew
When nothing is hidden, your actions are proof
In the light of pure love..

Do you gain from lessons life imparts?
And nourish a caring compassionate heart?
Are you eager to learn or do you live in the past?
To know thyself, do you travel that path?
In the light of pure love?

Do you adore your children and watch them grow?
With the wonder of life and emphatic sorrow?
Do you share their joy, give them hope for tomorrow?
Ease their troubles, give an example to follow?
In the light of pure love..

Does your genuine concern willingly extend
to the animal kingdom, the ocean and the land?
Does your sense of natures wonder innately expand?
And to all of Gods creatures is your intent to them?
In the light of pure love..

Are you true to your God in principle and morale?
Or is God just consulted when you're hurt or you fell?
Does your concept of God exist outside of yourself?
Or is God just a cynical story that sells?
In the light of pure love..

Do you understand that everything exists to a plan?
The world was created and the cosmos began
and continues to do as the universe expands?
In the unlimited eternity of all that can?
In the light of pure love..

Have you created a fate liable to excel?
Or will your karma create your personal hell?
Have you been touched by the angelic realms?
Has your efforts created the depth of a well
Of the light of pure love..

From the eyes of the world to the window of the soul
When you enter the other side from the time you borrow
Will you be bathed in the after glow?
Of a life well lived so that you eternally flow
In the light of pure love..

Ethereal Me

Written By Karen Muller

April 2018

I was as I am as I know I am now
I am standing in forever endowed
With the cast of life's many woes
To touch upon eternities flow
To meet as above, is to meet as below
As I learn and evolve to wisely grow
 To know thy shadow

Into the realms my mind does go
Illustrated simple images glow
I pause in the seconds that confound
And awareness fades from my surrounds
As I glimpse into eternities bounds
What is fathomable to expound
 Timelessness all around

Into vision intent from tomorrow
Future eyes are fleetingly borrowed
To see so far with my other sight
Irrelevant is time's endured might
As I connect to other worldly heights
In my personal intuitive plight
 Is intent with insight

My secret senses reveal to show
What is probable and what I can sow
With awareness in a prospective light
That grows in knowing increasingly bright
As day is to day and night is to night
As I beacon as I wish to invite
 Silence is might

I live in the moments that allows
Fleeting gifts, past lives avowed
My interaction with spirits abound
Free will living remembered, resounds
Reincarnation that the ghost in me astounds
To inter connection renowned
 Eternity so profound

Of being in the forever empowered
Knowingly rekindled and innately flowered
Faith and trust that love never dies
To passionately feel those in heavens skies
This magic does overwhelmingly surprise
To be so sensitively alive
 In God's divine omnipresent eyes

My Tears

Written By Karen Muller

August 2018

Do not judge my tears for they express the depth of my feelings when your words of wisdom spoken from the experience of your soul, embrace my heart.

Do not fear my tears for they tell of my loss, the part of me that processes the ever-changing evolving metamorphosis of living, dying and how to adjust.

Do not shun my tears as they emerge from the wonderment within that connects me to a fraction of magnificent divine essence, that overwhelms me.

Do not disrespect my tears as their silence does not echo hollowness but the richness of my life experience summed from my past, re-emerging in the now.

Do not disregard my tears as they express my vulnerable human suffering from the heartfelt pain from witnessing the demise of nature, from this amazingly beautiful world.

Do not dismiss my tears as they evolve from my ability to love and to love means to connect to the divine, to the spark of God, the Goddess, of all that is.

Do not ignore my tears as they touched upon you and made the connection to your own references of your emotions, for it is depth that is worth sharing.

Do not underestimate my tears as they have the ability to allow me to move forward with my emotions to create new space in the now and for time to come.

Do not simplify my tears as they have the ultimate power to process my inner world to allow the divine essence of healing to manifest and flow.

Water

Written By Karen Muller (Reynolds)
1979

Water, Oh wonderful elixir of life
Shine like a crystal, pyramid of light
Glowing with energy, glittering bright
Radiate through a prism, refraction of light
A polyhedron of hues of scintillating heights
Rainbows of colour such a beautiful sight
Twinkle with no form, flow as you might

Water, Oh wonderful elixir of power
From the river Nile to the cactus flower
As your fluent flow so easily scours
And to earth falls over minutes or hours
To reform those clouds that thunder and growl
Over these parched lands that you devour
Make raging torrents and the gentle showers

Water, Oh wonderful elixir of trial
The scorching deserts you beguile
From dewdrops to clouds you reconcile
Enhancing natures fragility, so volatile
On arid lands that stretch lifeless miles
Essential to all, in existence's survival
In seasons blessed with lands revival

Water, Oh wonderful elixir of earth
Entwining with nature divine is your worth
From invigorating penetration of dirt
To a joyous splash over the tumbling surf
Feel the blessed relief of a dry, parched thirst
You create tears of grief or tears of mirth
With gentle healing, your awareness gives birth

Wild Flower Morning

By Karen Muller (Reynolds)

1987

I want to be part of a wildflower morning

Amidst the fields with the sun a- dawning

I want to dance in the golden light rays

And spread my wings like a fairy fey

I want to smell the delicate perfumes

of scents released from sweet floral blooms

I want to be part of the new born day

Cast my troubles and cares away

I want to be part of the bird song forming

and flow with the sound in it's natural glory

I want to be part of breeze that whispers

the motions so gentle it shimmers and shivers

I want to be part of the colours so delicate

of natures wondrous life light palette

I want to be part of this joyous bouquet

Wash and refresh my soul every way

Mother Earth Father Sky

Written By Karen Muller

October 2018

Mother earth, Father sky
We are born your children
We have altered over time
Our true self is now hidden
Buried under a fragile facade
Is our reverent state of being
Our interconnection to you
Has become almost forbidden
We wallow in the novelty
Of the shallow social settings
Innately deep in poverty
Sacrificed by salary netting
To feed what is appearances
To give us a sense of meaning
The price is psychic severance
From truth and magic of living

Mother earth, Father sky
At this stage of modern time
Is forgotten our inner senses
We have chosen to be blind
If in honesty we look around
We would not believe our eyes
How living beauty that surrounds
Is watched as it slowly dies

In the ignorance is bidden
The triumph of material lies
The priority is to keep it going
Above all honourable rights
All focus on the fanatic defence
The money machine does grind
Our mortal habits destructive
In our worldly sacrifice

Mother earth, Father sky
The child was never sated
It grew to consider only self
It does not know the sacred
The child learnt how to destroy
The ethereal connection is wasted
To the living, the land, the sky and sea
Over time it is lacerated
The idea there is only the me
Is so selfishly appreciated
With utterly no compunction
We are what we created
Unto unnatural functioning
Influenced how the child is fated
Now devoid of the providential
We are no longer spiritually related

The Ocean

Written By Karen Muller

October 2018

Sliding grains between my toes
As I tread upon the golden shores
The heat of the sun flows to my feet
As I walk on through a cooling breeze
Salty sea air is enveloping me
The wind spray tosses the azure sea
As I amble to tread joyfully along
Every footprint sings an ancient song
Uniquely, newly formed and sung
Born on wet sand two becomes one
Washed away on a receding wave
Where I stood and shallow bathed
Ripples of wind form parallel bands
I see endless along the coastal sands
Sunlight reflects upon golden glitter
That turns into a silver shimmer
Sparkling effervescent lights
Stretch to touch forever heights
One reflection to bounce off the other
In balance and in the natural wonder
Of sky, life, sand and sea
This vastness is all a part of me
My heart does dance in this visions feast
And melds into a deep sense of release
All well being is lovingly increased
I breathe in this wonderful sight

Every thing in time is feeling right
The ever changing rhythm is more
The song of my Aquarian soul
Rejoicing in the grandeur of space
That gives again waves in breaths
I am deep in absorbing the profound
When flying gulls emit the sound
A cawing hunger does it cry
Circling in the infinite sky
Pure white wings reflect the sun
Moving in a circular span
Sheer luminescent reverie
To impress upon my memory
The oceans abundant gift of life
Underlines all evolution's might
Unseen forms of every type
Mysterious is the deep as dark as night
Then high in the translucent sky
As above is as below in tides
Refreshed and cleansed is my delight
My emotions soar to enduring heights
All combines with such a unique
Encompassing feeling of being free
Bliss in essence of soul felt ease
I gain a sense of enduring peace
As I twirl in a dance upon the beach

Whispers

Written By Karen Muller

March 21, 2018

From the very moment you were gone
My life it changed in all manner and form
My world destroyed can never be the same
I never knew there could be so much pain
If for only once I could cuddle you again
But my anguished desire is relived in vain
Then distinctly I heard you call my name
Your whispers said you are around
Your whispers did so clearly astound
Your whispers echoed in my surrounds

My heart it breaks, your memory so clear
Retraced in my mind, so precious so dear
When I remember how you had grown
All I am left with is all I have known
It tears me apart when I again fall upon
The sadness to which now I ever belong
In a world that has become so entirely wrong
Then your whispers urge me to go on
Then your whispers urge me to be strong
Then your whispers urge me to move along

I'm only left with our memories to keep
Inwardly emptiness sinks long and deep
My yearning for you is expressed by tears
As I desperately seek you standing near
To ease this ache, to know you are here
To comfort and attempt to allay my fears
That is when I sense your ethereal sphere
I hear you whisper you are not gone
I hear you whisper our love is as one
I hear you whisper of our eternal bond

I am caught in a life alone and fragile
My shattered world was once so agile
Then I remember each day brings us close
To a reunion but when we do not know
Although my mortality seems to have froze
I cannot undo what in this life I have chose
With the soaring highs and desperate lows
Then you whisper from the other dimension
Then you whisper that it is fates condition
Then you whisper that time is an illusion

There is no way out, I can't rise above
These feelings founded on deepest love
Destiny within our hearts we are bound
To fragile messages intense and profound
That echo like ripples that softly rebound
Through trusting the perceptible sound
Of the sweetest silence most tenderly found
I hear a whisper so tranquil and oh so mere
I hear a whisper through a veil delicately sheer
I hear a whisper from forever when you appear

There is no way around, above or below
We either diminish or together we grow
From my soul I know my intuition yields
Your fragile messages vividly alive and real
Expresses our spirituality together that seals
Sacred acquisition in this perceptive wheel
We are gifted the power of God's grace to heal
I hear your tranquil whisper meander so near
I hear your tranquil expression delicate and sheer
I feel angelic deep love when ever you appear

Shore's Embrace

Written By Karen Muller

September 2018

Rolling ocean waves
Is sounds of summer
That winter craved
Renewed in wonder
Awareness of
What time pervades
This sandy land
Formed from grains
Like no other
Where we bathed
With one another
Where daylight saves
We melted as lovers
With circling gulls
And swelling tides
We look into
Each others eyes
Took a moment to reflect
In memorable time
Of what is meant
By the depth

Of newness found
In natures bath
With ocean sounds
Waves crashed
They hit the sand
Eternal moments
Had began
To spark and stroke
Erotica's demands
That bestowed in us
What knowing can
Tumbling enhanced
A life long chance
Pulsating and growing
Together in this
Act of belonging
In salty embrace
On this rhythmic shore
We tasted forever
Forever more
The song of flow

From our eternal soul
As we tumbled into
Waves so deep
And into passion
Alive as this sea
Nirvana was sent
For us to keep
We came together
Wild and free
In a never ending
Rhythmic release
That procreated
Ecstatically
Where by time and tide
Met and formed
The meaning of life
To the oceans beat
Belonging forever
To you and me

The Void

Written By Karen Muller

November 2018

Vastness silent
Stillness timeless
I chance to wander
Through death's caress
Held spellbound
Mindfully obsessed
I hover
No more breath
I am the infant
In the beyond
Horizons gone
I live infinity
What I comprehend
Will never end
This black as deep
In the darkest night ink
It's limitless extent
To what I can think
This grey contrast
This sensory plight

As the bleakest dawn
In visual might
Where I am found
Where I am gone
What is meant
By this meaning beyond
As deep as this infinite space
This ultimate of profound
I have faced
Auguring death
Beyond forever
Hypnotic breathlessness
In the ether
Vast wonderment
Nothingness
Where all life and death resides
Where there is everything
Nothing abides
Where there is nothing
Devoid of life

Worded In A Wood

Written By Karen Muller

2018

Within loneliness, lies an instinctive peace

Where inner connection gives healing relief

In still quietness create a smooth empty space

From a world that is fast and materially based

Savour each moment, simply close your eyes

Discover nothingness, lose your sense of time

Even your breathing, slowing it down to a sigh

The goal is to empty thought, refresh your mind

Adjust for reflection on your endeavours in life

In moments find answers from your inner light

To compose natural solutions to help you abide

Thoughts worth considering, to give them a try

Allow pleasure and self compassion to unfold

You can clarify your dreams to reach your goals

In life's school learning through renewed insight

In the act of embracing true self worth to provide

Appreciation of your inner beauty of being just you

Combine the renewal and connect with your truth

Know what you can't change, what you can control

Is the way to connect and converse with your soul

That Moment

Written By Karen Muller
April 1986

In momentary breath
Hauntingly clear
Acquainted the sublime
Real and ancient

Endowed fleeting chance
Faith's familiarity
Has expressed the divine
Past judgement

An encounter that thence
Stirred memory
Of enigmatic paradigms
Blurred and distant

I die a thousand deaths
Falling obliviously
Through many lifetimes
In an instant

Healing

Written By Karen Muller
October 2018

The greatest known healers of our decade
Edgar Cayce, Harry Edwards and Louise Hay
Understood universal law of the healing force
That entwines everything and is a natural source
Through unwavering belief they did aggregate
With courage to inspire through profound faith
From their words, thoughts and altered states
Their legacy is enduring and largely calibrates
With the highest vibration the energy of love
As they willed to manifest and strove to prove
That now leaves an enduring inspiration for us
To believe in the power of conviction and trust

The gentleness of deep compassion can reach
To the soul of a person to enlighten and teach
We have an expansion of the interconnection
Even a smile unprompted is supportive action
Spontaneity from a stranger can be uplifting
By this genuine, emphatic expression of giving
Relief to lighten a burden, a heart heavy laden
Who knows what may potentially happen
Words spoken sincerely in heart felt kindness
Can break through a persons single mindedness
To help them to develop a broader life view
To comprehend a different perspective of truth

Words that are gifted in support and in wisdom
Can help another develop hopeful future vision
If there is lost aspiration or meaning for living
With your time, care and empathetic listening
Pain can be overcome by you simply perceiving
Another souls need with what they are struggling
To have the conviction to bravely speak out
To help another overcome debilitating doubt
Can aspire them to find what they innately seek
To safely subdue their sense of saddened defeat
You give hope for the future that may become
Restoration from dreams, broken and undone

Give from your heart at will and at random
Help others to understand to mindfully fathom
Change and free will is their right of living
And self- responsibility is just as empowering
It grants them the gift of gaining life's meaning
To successfully overcome that they are fearing
A heart felt wish or an implicit loving prayer
And visualising the person is healthy again
Is absent healing so simple yet it remains
Such a powerful medium to heal ones pain
Effective in the state of grace freely given
From spiritual energy the ultimate healing

With the gift of miraculous life force we share
Tools to ease life's trials, loss and despair
How you think will also have a great impact
On how you ameliorate and how you react
On the body, mind and your soul's operation
Your new thoughts provide you rejuvenation
You can surmount anything with determination
Any necessary answer is within your creation
Of welcome liberation and eventual relief
Foremost you must simply allow and believe
In a higher force that is powerful and free
Enabling to channel with abundance and ease

You may rely on angelic realms of vibration
Or endure by nature or God regeneration
Knowing the mind and body is so amazing
Feel the loss of energy and inertness abating
You have ability to become salubrious again
Because over time nothing remains the same
You facilitate if you focus on what you aspire
Anticipate on manifestation that you require
To nurse the way to live a life of your dreams
Through good health, intention and well being
To promote a healthy sense of inner freedom
And gain the benefits of giving and receiving

Printed in the United States
By Bookmasters